ABUNDANT TRUTH INTERNATIONAL MINISTRIES

Kingdom Stewards Series

D1572555

THE APOSTOLIC MINISTRY

Exploring the Apostolic Office and Gift

By: Roderick Levi Evans

Abundant Truth PUBLISHING
abundantpublishing.net
P.O. Box 126, Camden, NC 27921

Published by Abundant Truth Publishing
P.O. Box 126
Camden, NC 27921
Web: www.abundantpublishing.net
Email: abundantpublishing@gmail.com

Printed U.S.A.

Front & Back Cover Designs by Abundant Truth Publishing
U.S.A. All rights reserved.

Abundant Truth Publishing is a ministry of **Abundant Truth International Ministries.** The primary mission of ATI Ministries is to equip the Body of Christ with tools necessary to defend and contend for the truth of the Christian faith. Jesus Christ came to bear witness of the truth and ATI Ministries is a modern-day extension of His commission (John 18:37).

Kingdom Stewards – The Apostolic Ministry
©2005 Abundant Truth Publishing
All Rights Reserved

ISBN: 978-1-60141-047-4

Table of Contents

Introduction

Peter told the believers that they were *stewards* of the manifold grace of God. This means that every follower of Christ has the responsibility to grow and develop in their God-given gifts. In addition, they are to be faithful in ministering to others. The Kingdom Stewards Series was created to help believers understand their gifts and ministries. It is designed to bring clarity to the purpose and functions of spiritual gifts and ministries. It is our prayer that believers will grow in the recognition, acceptance, and operation of the gifts of God.

In this publication:

This publication presents a solid introduction to the apostolic ministry. It will bring clarity and understanding to the apostolic office, the apostolic anointing, and apostleship. This information will help individuals to recognize the operations of this anointing in their lives and in the lives of others. It is our hope that believers will develop a greater respect and appreciation for the apostolic office and gift.

1

What is an Apostle?

The first ministry to be on display in the New Testament Church was that of the apostle. The Book of Acts highlights the ministry of the apostles. Some biblical scholars have asserted that the only true apostles were the eleven disciples (excluding Judas Iscariot) with the exception of Paul. Others have stated that the ministry of the apostles is useless since we have the canon of scripture.

In addition, others promote that apostolic ministry ceased after the deaths of the first century apostles. As believers, we must understand that these teachings are erroneous. *The ministry of the apostle is still vital and important to the advancement of the kingdom of*

God and the Church. Without this ministry, the Church cannot fulfill its mission in the earth.

And He set some in the Church, first

apostles..(I Corinthians 12:28)

The word apostle originates from the Greek word *apostolos,* which means one who is sent forth. Apostles are sent from the presence of God with a divine message. They are sent forth for a specific task. Not all apostles will discharge their duty in the same manner; neither will they all have the same anointing.

Apostles' ministries will vary in demonstration and execution. Though apostolic ministry seems exclusive to the New Testament, we discover from the scriptures that apostolic ministry was demonstrated in the Old Testament.

Apostolic Ministry in the Old Testament

The apostolic ministry is a foundational ministry (will be discussed later). The apostolic anointing is designed to bring people into the knowledge of God and Christ. In the Old Testament, some men seemed to have an apostolic grace upon their lives.

Two key biblical figures that exemplify this truth are Abraham and Moses. Each of these men were prophets, but from God's interaction with them, we discover there was a type of apostolic anointing on their lives. They demonstrated three apostolic traits:

1) *They reflect the character of God.*
2) *They established individuals in the faith of God.*
3) *They exercised great spiritual authority and power.*

Abraham was sent to a foreign land by the command of God. Abraham received a commission as does an apostle.

Now the Lord had said unto Abram, Get

thee out of thy country, and from thy kindred, and from thy father's house, unto a land that I will shew thee. (Genesis 12:1)

The apostolic grace was evident in Abraham's life because it was through his life that foreigners were introduced to the God of heaven. The Lord magnified Himself in Abraham's life as he traveled throughout the land. We know that *Abraham's character reflected God's* as the apostle's does Christ. For God commanded him saying,

And when Abram was ninety years old and nine, the Lord appeared to Abram, and said unto him, I am the Almighty God; walk before me, and be thou perfect. (Genesis 17:1)

Like the modern day apostle, *Abraham was used to establish the faith of God* in his descendants and in the earth. As apostles are fathers in the Spirit, Abraham is the father of faith.

> *And God said unto Abraham, Thou shalt keep my covenant therefore, thou, and thy seed after thee in their generations. (Genesis 17:9)*

Finally, Abraham exercised great authority and power. After God rebuked Abimelech for Sarah's sake, He told the king that Abraham would pray for him and the barrenness of his household would end. As apostles exercise great power, so did Abraham through his prayer.

> *So Abraham prayed unto God: and God healed Abimelech, and his wife, and his maidservants; and they bare children. For the Lord had fast closed up all the wombs of the house of Abimelech, because of Sarah Abraham's wife. (Genesis 20;17-18)*

Moses, like Abraham demonstrated apostolic grace. When God spoke of his ministry,

He said that Moses was not like other prophets. *Apostles and prophets are similar, but the apostle's ministry is greater than the prophet's because of the spiritual authority of the office.* This is what Moses represented in his day. He was a prophet, but there was something greater about him.

> *And he said, Hear now my words: If there be a prophet among you, I the Lord will make myself known unto him in a vision, and will speak unto him in a dream. My servant Moses is not so, who is faithful in all mine house. (Numbers 12:6-7)*

When God sent Moses to Pharaoh, He told Moses that Aaron would be his prophet, and Moses would be as God to Pharaoh. This is a clear demonstration of the apostolic grace. Moses would reflect God's character as he fulfilled his ministry. Numerous biblical accounts recall the power that Moses exercised. Signs and wonders surrounded his ministry to the Jews. This is parallel to the ministry of the apostles.

Finally, like the modern day apostle, Moses established people in the faith of God. The apostles laid a spiritual foundation for the Church to grow upon while Moses instituted the Law from God to set up the Levitical priesthood and Israelite worship.

From these two patriarchs, we see a demonstration and foreshadowing of the apostolic ministry to come under the New Covenant.

Apostolic Ministry in the New Testament

After the establishment of the Church, God used apostles. *The apostle is sent as a chief representative of Christ.* They represent the person of Christ to the Church and world (however, this is done alongside other believers and ministers). They are preachers of the Gospel of Jesus Christ.

Apostles mature believers in their walks with the Lord. They serve as spiritual fathers. They have the grace upon their lives to establish order to the worship of God. In addition, they have prophetic insight and great authority in the realm of the Spirit.

In addition to the above functions, the New Testament apostle serves as a foundational ministry to the Church. On the day of Pentecost, God established His will for man's worship. He no longer wanted to be "confined" to a building (represented by God's command to worship at the Temple), but dwell in the hearts of man. His will was for the believer to be His temple.

As He abides in each individual, they corporately become the temple of God. Peter called the believers "stones" who are built together to form a spiritual house or temple where God could dwell.

> *Ye also, as lively stones, are built up a spiritual house, an holy priesthood, to offer up spiritual sacrifices, acceptable to God by Jesus Christ. (I Peter 2:5)*
>
> *What? Know ye not that your body is the temple of the Holy Ghost which is in you, which ye have of God, and ye are not your own? (I Corinthians 6:19)*

With the New Covenant, the temple of God is now the hearts and minds of people. Their actual bodies become the habitation of God. Therefore, if the Church consists of people joined together by the presence of the Holy Spirit, then the foundation for the Church would consist of people.

As Paul wrote to the believers, he revealed to them a very important truth. He told them that they (the Church) were built upon the foundation of the **apostles** and prophets with Christ being the head stone.

> *Now therefore ye are no more strangers and foreigners, but fellowcitizens with the saints, and of the household of God; And are built upon the foundation of the apostles and prophets, Jesus Christ himself being the chief corner stone; In whom all the building fitly framed together groweth unto an holy temple in the Lord: In whom ye also are builded together for an habitation of God through the Spirit. (Ephesians 2:19-22).*

In the above scripture, we discover certain truths. Paul was writing to a primarily Gentile audience. However, we must understand that the foundation that they stood upon was the same as the Jewish believers. Jewish and Gentile believers, alike, operated in the foundation established by the New Testament **apostles** and prophets.

The Church, like the New Covenant, was founded upon people, namely, the **apostles** and prophets. From this, we understand that since we will reign with Christ, God allowed man to have an active role in the establishment of the Church.

The **apostles** and prophets bear the responsibility for the Church, especially in doctrinal purity and spiritual direction. As Christ formed the foundation for the New Covenant, the **apostles** and prophets formed the foundation for the Church.

Their ministries are foundational and continue to be major influences upon the Body of Christ.

The ministries of the **apostles** and prophets were needed to establish the Church, and their ministries are needed presently for the furtherance of the Church. Christ's ministry toward us is everlasting.

But this man, because he continueth ever, hath an unchangeable priesthood. Wherefore he is able also to save them to the uttermost that come unto God by him, seeing he ever liveth to make intercession for them. (Hebrews 7:24-25)

The Book of Acts reveals to us that the ministries of the apostles were essential in the establishment of the Church and the advancement of the Kingdom of God.

Consider the following:

Signs and wonders accompanied the apostles' ministries to confirm the message that they preached. This helps to advance the Kingdom of God.

And fear came upon every soul: and many wonders and signs were done by the apostles. (Acts 2:43)

God also bearing them witness, both with

signs and wonders, and with divers miracles, and gifts of the Holy Ghost, according to his own will. (Hebrews 2:4)

The apostles' ministries were vital to establishing the Church and believers in the faith.

And they continued stedfastly in the apostles' doctrine and fellowship, and in breaking of bread, and in prayers. (Acts 2:42)

This second epistle, beloved, I now write unto you; in both which I stir up your pure minds by way of remembrance: That ye may be mindful of the words which were spoken before by the holy prophets, and of the commandment of us the apostles of the Lord and Saviour. (2 Peter 3:1-2)

Not only did the New Testament apostles reveal future events and encourage the brethren, but also they helped to set up elders and pastors in the Church.

> *For this cause left I thee in Crete, that thou shouldest set in order the things that are wanting, and ordain elders in every city, as I had appointed thee. (Titus 1:5)*

From the above scriptures and references, we discover that the New Testament Church has apostles, individuals who possess as apostolic anointing, and those who have and apostolic gift. These gifts were needed then and they are needed now.

There are some theologians who twist the scriptures. They assert that because we have the canon of scripture, apostles and apostolic ministry are no longer needed. The scriptures declare that Jesus Christ is the same yesterday, today, and forever (Hebrews 13:8). He ministered to the early Church through the apostles. He will not change until the end of all things.

If He used apostles and apostolic ministry in those times, He will continue to do so. Christ's ministry to the Church will not end until the Judgment; therefore, the ministries of the apostles will not end until that Day. God is still using apostles today. In addition, God is raising up individuals who walk under and in an apostolic anointing that His glory may be seen in all.

2

The Office of the Apostle

We will now explore the apostle's role in the Church. There is a diversity in the demonstration and expression of apostolic ministry. Apostolic ministry manifests itself in various ways. However, there is some common ground among all apostles. No matter what their specific call is, apostles will exhibit characteristics of ambassadors, fathers, and husbands as they minister in the Church.

Apostles as Ambassadors

Every apostle is unique in his ministry. However, the apostle's role in the kingdom of God may parallel an ambassador's role in any earthly kingdom. Ambassadors are important to any nation. Oftentimes, they carry the nation's peace, prosperity, and safety by their words and actions. Though every member of the Body of Christ functions as an ambassador for Him at some time, it is the primary role of the apostle. Paul compared apostolic ministry to that of an ambassador.

> *So, we as Christ's ambassadors, God making His appeal as it were through us. We {as Christ's personal representative} beg you for His sake to lay hold of the divine power [now offered you] and be reconciled to God. (II Corinthians 5:20 Amplified)*

Ambassadors are the highest officials and/or representatives in government. The word translated ambassador in the New Testament comes from the Greek word "presbeuo." It means to be a senior representative. Therefore, we conclude that among those God call into ministry, the apostle is the senior representative of the kingdom of God.

God set the apostles in the Church first, so that they could function as the ambassadors of the kingdom of God to the world's kingdom. They above all the other ministers must represent the kingdom of God as if Christ were still in the earth.

Ambassadors are sent forth with specific guidelines of the one who sent them. An ambassador does not choose what his assignment is. The ruler or government decides this. An ambassador does not become or function as an ambassador unless designated. The same is true for the apostle. The Lord appoints an apostle.

Individuals cannot lay claim to this office because of gifts, talents, and the advice of men. Jesus chose the apostles. If someone feels called to this office, the Lord will make it clear. However, one must remember that every apostle has a specific call on his life. Though he has great authority, only God directs him as to how to administer it.

Ambassador's influence is limited to that given by ruler or government. An ambassador only has influence in the countries that his government gives him. For instance, an ambassador to China may not have the same influence in Japan, if not sanctioned by the sending government.

Apostles only have authority over what God gives them. An apostle over one organization cannot assume apostleship over any organization or people in the Kingdom of God. God, alone, gives him his sphere of influence.

Some apostolic ministers have ignored this fact and tried to usurp authority in churches and organizations where the Lord has not sent them. The apostle only has authority and influence in the places where God has sent them.

Ambassador's words are equal to the one that sent them. When ambassadors are commissioned, they are to speak as the ruler or government. Wars have begun and ended because of decisions made by the ambassadors.

Above all the other offices, the apostles are to represent the voice of Christ and be in his stead as they minister in the Church. Apostles are expected to speak and act even as Christ would. Apostles have to possess the nature of Christ. The apostle's actions have to be a reflection of the mind of Christ operating in them. (I Corinthians 2:16)

Ambassadors have an invested/inherent authority. Ambassadors are sent out with all authority and power of the commissioning government. Since they stand in place of the governing leadership, they walk in their power. Ambassadors are given this authority that they may fulfill their commission. Ambassadors cannot assume authority that is not given to them.

Apostles also have an invested authority. Their authority does not come because of what they do or who they are. Apostles do not have authority because they are apostles, but because God gives it to them. Apostles have to resist the temptation to abuse the authority God gives them.

> *For though I should boast somewhat more of our authority, which the Lord hath given us for edification, and not for your destruction, I should not be ashamed. (II Corinthians 10:8)*

If apostles abuse their authority, it will result in the destruction of the Body of Christ. There are numerous accounts in the Church today of apostles who misuse their power.

Ambassadors are expected to have wisdom, counsel, and knowledge of their ruler. Ambassadors are entrusted with the responsibility of representing those who sent them. Therefore, the training and discipline placed upon them is great. They must have personal integrity and character. In addition, they must be able to represent those who have commissioned them with knowledge and dignity.

Apostles are no different. They, too, must possess the wisdom, knowledge, and personality of Christ. Because they walk in the very authority of Christ, the training and discipline of God is oftentimes grave. This is so that when they speak, they will speak as an oracle of God, even more so, they will speak in Christ's stead.

Apostles as Fathers

The role of an apostle in the Church is not only to be an ambassador for Christ, but also to serve as a "father" ministry. The apostle's role in the kingdom is similar to that of a father. The apostles, themselves, referred to themselves as fathers and to those who partook of their ministry as their children. While writing to the Corinthian church, Paul likened his ministry unto a father. John called the saints his children.

> *For if you were to have countless tutors in Christ, yet you would not have many fathers; for in Christ Jesus I became your father through the gospel. (I Corinthians 4:15 NASV)*

> *My little children, these things write I unto you, that ye sin not. And if any man sin, we have an advocate with the Father, Jesus Christ the righteous. (I John 2:1)*

The apostle will love the Church as a father loves his children. His personality in the Church will resemble that of a father.

Fathers provide for their children. As an earthly father provides for the needs of his children, the apostle will supply the spiritual needs of those entrusted to him. He will endeavor to ensure that the Church has the right information to live in this world in victory. They will strive to lay proper foundations in the lives of the people of God; that they may inherit the kingdom of God. Paul wrote,

> Behold, the third time I am ready to come to you; and I will not be burdensome to you: for I seek not yours, but you: for the children ought not to lay up for the parents, but the parents for the children. And I will very gladly spend and be spent for you; though the more abundantly I love you, the less I be loved. (II Corinthians 12:14-15)

He explained to those at Corinth that as a father works and provides (spends) for his children, so he labors and expends his time, energy, and effort to provide for them spiritually. He wanted their souls to be saved. Apostles have to avoid becoming "lord" and "kings" over the people of God. God has set them in the Church to serve.

Fathers nurture their children. Though a father provides for his children, provision without nurture handicaps a child. An apostle must not only labor in the Church, his labor has to be goal oriented. Whatever the apostle's specific call is, his concern will be a personal one.

> But I (Paul and other apostles) proved to be gentle among you, as a nursing mother tenderly cares for her own children. (I Thessalonians 2:7 NASV, Parenthesis mine)

The apostle's personal concern has to be tempered with grace and patience. Because God uses them to bring order and stability, some apostles become harsh in their words and demeanor. The anointing of God is not to be blamed for character flaws.

Fathers discipline their children. If a child has no discipline or training, he is liable to develop into a corrupt adult. The same is true for believers. If Christians are not disciplined, they will not grow up into mature saints.

Apostles will execute judgment and discipline in the Church. However, love is to be the motivation for the rebuke. John demonstrated this apostolic authority in his third epistle.

> For this reason, if I come, I will call attention to his deeds which he does, unjustly accusing us with the wicked words; and not satisfied with this, neither does he himself receive the brethren, and he forbid those who desire to do so, and puts them out of the Church. (3 John verse 10 NASV)

John says that he will "call attention" to what a divisive minister did. He was expressing that he would personally deal with the individual because of his error.

Paul, on numerous occasions, exercised judgment and meted out discipline in the Church. While away from Corinth, news reached him that a brother was sleeping with this stepmother. He not only rebuked the church for not handling the situation, but also gave instruction concerning the discipline of the brother.

It is reported commonly that there is fornication among you, and such fornication as is not so much as named among the Gentiles, that one should have his father's wife. And ye are puffed up, and have not rather mourned, that he that hath done this deed might be taken away from among you. For I verily, as absent in body, but present in spirit, have judged already, as though I were present, concerning him that hath so done this deed, In the name of our Lord Jesus Christ, when ye are gathered together, and my spirit, with the power of our Lord Jesus Christ, To deliver such an one unto Satan for the destruction of the flesh, that the spirit may be saved in the day of the Lord Jesus. (I Corinthians 5:1-5)

Paul meted out discipline. However, it was for the salvation of the offender. True fathers discipline their children to save them. When the apostle rebukes, it has to be done in love, else he will offend one of God's very own. He must remember that he has a Father in heaven.

Fathers give wise/sound instruction to their children. The book of Proverbs is a compilation of instructions that a father would give to his children. Fathers seek to instill knowledge in their children. A father will pass on the information that he has learned. Apostles will impart revelation and knowledge to the Church as a father does to his children.

> *And they continued stedfastly in the apostles' doctrine and fellowship, and in breaking of bread, and in prayers. (Acts 2:42)*

> *But, beloved, remember ye the words which were spoken before of the apostles of our Lord Jesus Christ. (Jude verse17)*

The Church was established on the apostle's teaching. Peter instructed them to remember what had been previously taught. He did not cite the teaching of other elders and leaders, but what the apostles taught. Apostles are expected to give fatherly wisdom and instruction in the Church.

Nine Functions of the Apostle

Though there are varieties of ministries and operations, apostles have essentially the same functions. Some functions are not exclusive to apostles. However, apostles will differ from other ministries in the execution of those functions.

Preach & Teach the Word of God (I Tim. 2:7). Apostles are gifted to preach and/or teach the word of God under divine inspiration and authority. They are anointed to make known the mysteries of God through the Word. This is performed with boldness and sobriety.

> Let a man so account of us (apostles), as of the ministers of Christ, and stewards of the mysteries of God. (I Corinthians 4:1 Parenthesis mine)

Impart Spiritual Gifts (Acts 8:17; Romans 1:11; II Tim. 1:6). Apostles have the ability to bring forth the gifts of God in believers. They have the power to impart wisdom, knowledge, and understanding. Apostles can bring to light the spiritual gifts resident in believers and impart gifts (by revelation of the Spirit) through the laying on of hands.

> *Neglect not the gift that is in thee, which was given thee by prophecy, with the laying on of the hands of the presbytery. (I Timothy 4:14)*

Establish and/or Oversee Churches and Organizations. Because apostles are sent with a divine message, God uses some to start organizations as vehicles to present their messages. In addition, apostles will start new churches and ministries in areas where they are sent to preach. This is to give structure to those who have heard the message. For example, Paul and Barnabas started many churches to give the new converts some organization to the worship of

God.

> *And some days after Paul said unto Barnabas, Let us go again and visit our brethren in every city where we have preached the word of the Lord, and see how they do. (Acts 15:36)*

Evangelize. Every apostle has a message. Apostles are gifted to go into areas that have not been open to the gospel or areas that are stagnant. Jesus sent the original twelve out to preach. Every apostle will function as an evangelist, whether to the Church (to bring balance and order) or to the Lost (for redemption and salvation).

> *For so hath the Lord commanded us, saying, I have set thee to be a light of the Gentiles, that thou shouldest be for salvation unto the ends of the earth. And when the Gentiles heard this, they were glad, and glorified the word of the Lord: and as many*

as were ordained to eternal life believed. And the word of the Lord was published throughout all the region. (Acts 13:47-49)

Raise Up Leaders (Acts 15:39; II Tim. 2:1-2; Acts 6:3-6). Because of the authority given to them, apostles have the anointing and responsibility to raise up leaders. This is done for the advancement of the kingdom of God.

Apostles will have "Timothys" and "Elishas" in ministry so that the work of the Lord will continue after they have left the scene. If an apostle is the head of a religious organization, he will have the ability to recognize gifts and ministries in individuals and set them in the Church as directed by the Spirit.

To Titus, mine own son after the common faith: Grace, mercy, and peace, from God the Father and the Lord Jesus Christ our Saviour. For this cause left I thee in Crete, that thou shouldest set in order the things that are wanting, and ordain elders in every city, as I had appointed thee. (Titus 1:4-5)

Expose False Apostles & Doctrine. Apostles are stewards of over the mysteries of God. They have the wisdom and foresight to warn against deception. They will contend for purity of faith and doctrine in the Church. They, like the prophets of old, will warn and speak against false apostles openly.

But there were false prophets also among the people, even as there shall be false teachers among you, who privily shall bring in damnable heresies, even denying the Lord that bought them, and bring upon themselves swift destruction. And many shall follow their pernicious ways; by reason of whom the way of truth shall be evil spoken of. (II Peter 2:1-2)

Perform Signs, Wonders, Healings, & Miracles. The apostle has a miraculous ministry. Apostles are gifted men, not only to perform signs and wonders, but in the revelation gifts of the Spirit. The word of knowledge, word of wisdom, discerning of spirits, and prophecy will operate regularly in their ministries.

> *And fear came upon every soul; and many wonders and signs were done by the apostles. (Acts 2:43)*

Lay Spiritual Foundations in the Church. Apostles have the authority and anointing to lay spiritual foundations in the Church. Though no modern-day apostles will write scripture, they are equipped to reveal the hidden truths of God's Word and lay the proper foundation for the people of God to grow thereby.

> *Whereby, when ye read, ye may understand my knowledge in the mystery of Christ)*

which in other ages was not made known unto the sons of men, as it is now revealed unto his holy apostles and prophets by the Spirit. (Ephesians 3:4-5)

Establish Churches in the Faith (Gospel). Apostles have the unique ability to bring people back to the purity of the faith. They are able to instruct babes in Christ until they become mature in their personal relationships with God and in their doctrinal beliefs. They can promote stability and growth in the Body of Christ.

And as they went through the cities, they delivered them the decrees for to keep, that were ordained of the apostles and elders which were at Jerusalem. And so were the churches established in the faith, and increased in number daily. (Acts 16:4-5)

Though there are many dimensions to this awesome ministry (not listed), most apostles will demonstrate all of these functions at some time in their ministries.

3

What is Apostleship?

"I have an apostolic anointing." "I have been called as an apostle." "I am an apostle." These are expressions that are increasingly heard in the Body of Christ. Some believers are put off by them. Though some individuals who say this may be in error, God has placed the apostolic gift in the Body of Christ. It is not only reserved for those who are apostles, but for any believer whom the Spirit will endow.

The apostolic grace is a widely misunderstood gift; so, many are still confused about its use, function, and purpose. In this chapter, we want to discover the fullness of the apostolic gift and ministry in the Body of Christ. The totality of apostolic ministry is described in one word: *apostleship.* It is a term used by Paul to describe his ministry.

> *By whom we have received grace and apostleship, for obedience to the faith among all nations, for his name. (Romans 1:5)*

However, apostleship is something that the Spirit will give to whom He will. The word *apostleship* means commission. There are individuals in the Body of Christ who are not apostles, but have a commission from God.

God operates in diversity. There are different aspects of apostleship demonstrated in the Body of Christ. There are levels to apostleship. As we discuss each, we will understand the purpose of apostleship in the Church.

The Apostolic Gift

In its simplest form, again, apostleship is a commission. There are individuals in the Body of

Christ who have received a specific commission from the Lord. Individuals who receive such a commission share in the first level of apostleship. They have an apostolic gift.

The apostolic gift manifests in different ways. Ministers who have an apostolic gift will oftentimes start churches and religious organizations by the command of the Lord. They may not be apostles, but they will be sent to certain areas to pastor or start organizations whereby the Kingdom of God advances. However, after the church is planted and the organization established, the apostolic gift takes a 'back seat' to the calling on their lives.

In the laity, individuals who have an apostolic gift will start departments and auxiliaries in their churches. They will have vision to see the local assembly grow. They will be faithful members in service.

Aside from organizational skills and abilities, anyone who has an apostolic gift will, at times, exercise authority in the Spirit. They will also demonstrate the power of God. They will be spiritually sensitive men and women who have only a desire to please Christ.

The Apostolic Anointing

There are individuals in the Church who are not apostles, but there is a definite apostolic touch on their lives and ministries. These individuals are said to possess an apostolic anointing. This is the next level of apostleship. How does this differ from someone who has an apostolic gift? In simple terms, the person who has an apostolic gift will demonstrate apostolic grace and ability occasionally.

However, an individual with an apostolic anointing will demonstrate apostolic power, grace, and authority regularly as they minister to the Body of Christ. Possessing an apostolic anointing does not place one in the office of the apostle, but it does make them a part of the emerging apostolic company of believers.

The apostolic anointing is seen oftentimes in believers who are called to the five-fold ministry. They will operate in their respective offices while exercising apostolic power and authority. The apostolic anointing adds a depth and dimension to their ministries. In addition, one does not have to be called to a ministry office to possess an apostolic anointing (discussed earlier). These individuals are strategically placed in the Body of Christ that all may be partakers of the apostolic ministry.

Individuals who possess an apostolic anointing will manifest the revelation and power of the Spirit consistently. They will have encounters with the Lord frequently. This may be in dreams and visions or in visitations of the Holy Spirit. In addition, they will be able to help others grow in their relationship with the Lord. Some will function like missionaries (sent ones) between churches. They will travel from assembly to assembly, strengthening pastors and leadership through their service.

The next manifestation of the apostolic spirit is, of course, **The Apostolic Office,** which is the focus of this book. We shall go on to the next level of the apostolic ministry in the Church.

The Apostolic Spirit

The greatest expression of apostleship is not in the apostolic gift, the apostolic anointing, or the ministry of the apostle. It is in the apostolic spirit. The early Church was effective because they appreciated and accepted the ministry of the apostles. As a result, great grace and power rested upon the thousands of believers in Jerusalem.

And they continued stedfastly in the apostles' doctrine and fellowship, and in breaking of bread, and in prayers. And fear came upon every soul: and many wonders and signs were done by the apostles. And all that believed were together, and had all things common; And sold their possessions and goods, and parted them to all men, as every man had need. And they, continuing daily with one accord in the temple, and breaking bread from house to house, did eat their meat with gladness and singleness of heart, Praising God, and having favour with all the people. And the Lord added to the church daily such as should be saved. (Acts 2:42-47)

The early Church demonstrated the apostolic spirit. This is the highest level of apostleship. Jesus' words to the apostles illustrate the manifestation of the apostolic spirit.

> *Go ye therefore, and teach all nations, baptizing them in the name of the Father, and of the Son, and of the Holy Ghost: Teaching them to observe all things whatsoever I have commanded you: and, lo, I am with you alway, even unto the end of the world. Amen. (Matthew 28:19-20)*

In the Gospels, Jesus gives a charge to the apostles before He ascended. It is understood that the charge given to them is one that the Church is to fulfill corporately.

> *Go ye therefore, and teach all nations, baptizing them in the name of the Father, and of the Son, and of the Holy Ghost: Teaching them to observe all things whatsoever I have commanded you: and, lo, I am with you alway, even unto the end of the world. Amen. (Matthew 28:19-20)*

The Church is sent to the world to represent Christ. The apostolic spirit represents the Church's apostleship to the world. How does this affect the local assembly? When an assembly embraces the apostolic spirit, three things are evident. They are the same things that were evident in the early Church.

1. **Unity** – When the apostolic spirit is manifested in an assembly, every believer will operate in love and support of one another. The sign of a true follower of Christ is love. Love, in turn, produces unity.

> *By this shall all men know that ye are my disciples, if ye have love one to another. (John 13:35)*

Since God and Christ are love, the apostolic spirit compels believers to work together in unity. The unity produced through the apostolic spirit sets the stage for the manifestation of power in the Church.

2. **Power** – The assembly walking under an apostolic spirit will be a place of healing, deliverance, and salvation. The miraculous will be seen daily in the life of that church. The least to the greatest among the people will demonstrate the power of God in healing the sick, casting out of devils, and effective evangelism.

> *And these signs shall follow them that believe; In my name shall they cast out devils; they shall speak with new tongues; They shall take up serpents; and if they drink any deadly thing, it shall not hurt them; they shall lay hands on the sick, and they shall recover. (Mark 16:17-18)*

3. **Expansion of the Kingdom of God** – After unity and power, the church flowing in the apostolic spirit will cause expansion in the Kingdom. The assembly will grow, not because of other believers

coming to fellowship. It will grow because souls will be added daily to the Kingdom because of the power and love expressed. In turn, the assembly will be a force in its city, county, and state because of the apostolic spirit.

> *And the Lord added to the church daily such as should be saved. (Acts 2:47b)*

The apostolic spirit is something that every fellowship of believers should seek for. The early Church had it and the Lord prospered them. If we possess it, we will see the miraculous of the Books of Acts today. In addition, the Kingdom of God will advance. Now that we have discussed the different aspects of apostleship, we have created a diagram showing the different levels in apostleship. The apostolic progression from the apostolic gift to the apostolic spirit is comparable to a flight of steps. The only way to go higher, one has to climb the steps. If the Church appreciates the apostolic gift, apostolic anointing, and apostolic office, we will experience the apostolic spirit in our day.

The apostolic spirit will only manifest as the apostleship of the believers and apostles is accepted and received. The apostolic spirit is something the entire Church is to possess.

As the Church embraces (accepts and acknowledges) each manifestation of the apostolic, it moves a step closer to becoming apostolic corporately, culminating with the Church fulfilling its commission given by Christ to the apostles.

Guidelines for Judging the Apostolic

One of the major facets of understanding apostleship is to discern when something is not apostolic. Judging the apostolic can be a tough task at times. Nevertheless, there are guidelines to help us as we strive to receive those with this gift and anointing. We need the apostolic in the Church, but some of us have lost faith in the apostolic gift and ministry. If you are unsure as to what and who is apostolic, there are certain questions you can ask yourself.

We must understand that God is the giver of the apostolic grace. We do not need to be afraid, but discerning. Even if we have heard or seen individuals misrepresent the apostolic office and gift, we should not allow the enemy to steal a blessing from us. God may be trying to even birth an apostolic gift in you or send someone with this anointing for your benefit.

Is the individual humble? Those with an apostolic calling and gift will be humble. They will know that without God, they can do nothing. They will consistently turn the people's attention to Christ and not themselves.

But God forbid that I should glory, save in the cross of our Lord Jesus Christ, by whom the world is crucified unto me, and I unto the world. (Galatians 6:14)

Conversely, do not be quick to say someone does not have this gift or anointing because of character flaws. Apostles and apostolic individuals grow in grace and character as other believers.

Is their doctrine sound and full of wisdom? Those with an apostolic gift (ministers or not) will have a clear understanding of the scriptures. They will be able to present the word of God with clarity. They will continue to develop their doctrine because they respect God and His word. They desire that all understand God's truth through the scriptures

On the other hand, there are apostolic individuals who have a valid gift, but they are in the middle of God's process of perfecting. They still may be on the potter's wheel. Some may try to operate in this anointing and gift before time. This may contribute to elementary or erroneous doctrine.

Do they follow leadership? Apostolic individuals will respect and follow leadership. Christ came in submission to the Father. Apostolic individuals will support leadership. They know that this is pleasing to Christ.

Individuals who find it hard to follow leadership may not have sat at the foot of Christ. One sign of an apostolic call is that they follow Christ. To follow Christ is to follow His example. He ministered in submission to the Father. The apostolic individual will minister in subjection to leadership.

Is there a manifestation of authority and power in the Spirit of God? Part of the apostolic call is the working of the miraculous power of

God. Any individual claiming an apostolic gift or anointing should show some level of giftedness by the Spirit and results in ministering. There should be testimonies of salvation, healing, and deliverance from others concerning them.

Is there confirmation of the apostolic call or gift? God is not the author of confusion. He does not work against Himself. He will not give a gift or calling without providing some form of confirmation in the Body. Even if your gift is not specifically stated, there will be a recognition of the grace that is upon your life. However, if an individual is claiming the apostolic office, there will be confirmation (usually by elders and apostles) of the ministry.

Shun away from individuals claiming an apostolic call and no one else knows about it. Usually, these individuals are self-willed. They demonstrate little power. Oftentimes, they are not faithful or accountable to anyone.

*For a full examination of the ministry of the apostle which expands on the information in this brief study, I recommend my other book entitled, **"The Apostle Question: Exploring the Role of Apostles in the New Testament Church."**

Made in the USA
Las Vegas, NV
30 January 2022

42648006R00037